You GO!

Discovering the Place
Where Your Garden Lives

Greg Peterson

Urban Farm Press
Phoenix, AZ

Grow Wherever You Go!

Discovering the Place
Where Your Garden Lives
Copyright © 2009 by Greg Peterson. All Rights Reserved.

No part of this book may be reproduced in any form, or by any electronic or mechanical means, including information storage and retrieval systems, without permission in writing from the author. The only exception is by a reviewer, who may quote short excerpts in a review.

Cover design - Parri Willie & Bethany Fisher
Cover layout - Bethany Fisher
Editing - Kathy Davidson, Kaylie Nykai

First Printing: November 2009
ISBN 978-0-9841788-3-4

For speaker information or to purchase books wholesale contact:
Urban Farm Press
5555 N 7th Street • Suite 134-144
Phoenix, AZ 85014 • 602-279-3713
http://www.UrbanFarmPress.com

Inspired by the Messenger Mini-Books

Grow Wherever You Go!

Sign up today for our
educational email series
15 Essentials to
Living a Green Lifestyle

Living a green lifestyle comes with a lot of choices, many of them confusing. How do you trust what a company claims about a product? Author Greg Peterson has created a series of emails designed to inspire you into your own level of greenness. His number one rule is "no suffering allowed!" For more information visit: www.YourGuideToGreen.com/15

****

The Urban Farm's
Simple Sustainability Book Series
is available for
purchase online at
YourGuideToGreen.com

This Book is Unique!

The Messenger Mini-Book you are holding is connected to an online technology that continues the message in this book through a FREE online environment. You will find expanded content on the message, audio and video clips, graphics, pictures and links to resources related to this book.

If you want a deeper, personalized experience of this book's message, go to the link below and input the book's ID number. You can then access the extended resources of this book provided to you by the author for FREE. Enjoy the journey!

Go to:
www.MessengerMiniBooks.com
ID#: 272731

Grow Wherever You Go!

Table of Contents

Introduction	. . .7
Urban Farm Possibilities	. .13
Shifting to Edibles	. .15
Just Observe	. .19
Getting Started	. .25
Building Healthy Soil	. .27
What's In A Seed?	. .33
Urban Farm Models	. .39
Ready, Set...Grow	. .47
Your Stories	
I Am an Urban Farmer	. .51
My Fire Escape Garden	. .52
1933 New Deal	. .54
Returning Home	. .57
Community Refugee Garden	. .62
My Instant Garden	. .67
Pool Side Fish Farmer	. .70
Balcony Fish Farming	. .73
It is My Little Garden of Eden	. .78
Ready, Fire, Aim	. .82
My Urban Herb Garden	. .87
Eating Wild	. .89

Introduction

This book is about innovative solutions for growing our own local and organic food. I believe that virtually everyone has the ability to either grow some food at home, or to find an appropriate location to start a garden. I may sound like a kook who plants my landscape with cucumbers instead of carnations, peppers instead of petunias, and fruit trees rather than ficus, but I am convinced that wherever you go, you can grow food! Now is the time for us to join together and plant the seeds that will transform the places in which we live.

I envision a day when every city and town has community gardens and growing spaces, nurtured into life by neighbors who are no longer strangers, but friends who delight in the edible rewards offered from a garden they discovered together. Imagine small strips of land between apartment buildings that have been turned into vegetable gardens, and urban orchards planted at schools and churches to grow food for our communities. The seeds of the urban farming movement already are growing within our reality. Throughout the world there are individuals, schools, community gardens, and houses of worship that have benefited from growing their own fruits and vegetables or acquiring food locally.

The chefs at one well-known corporate cafeteria made a commitment to purchase only foods that are grown within a 150-mile radius of their location. When they realized they couldn't get lemons or limes nearby, they planted trees and grew their own. While lemon trees may not grow everywhere, lemon verbena or lemon grass provide a tasty substitute and can be grown where lemons cannot.

Many people and organizations around the country already are growing food in nontraditional places and I will share some of their successes and struggles. Within these pages I also talk about my own efforts to raise food in an urban setting. This book ranges from the philosophical to the practical and includes tips for all types of living situations, from turning apartment patios into herb gardens to transforming suburban lawns into productive and beautiful organic vegetable gardens and urban fruit orchards. I have no doubt that once you've discovered your garden, you'll want to share the fruits of your labors.

Aside from experiencing the fulfillment of growing your own food, gardening offers an expanded relationship with the world around us. By growing and eating what is in season you also get a fresh and more nutritious meal. On a deeper level, the act of cultivating plants throughout the year allows us to experience nature firsthand: the ebb and flow of the life cycle; the far-reaching benefits of rainwater; and the regenerative power of seeds that develop into heads of broccoli, lettuce, tomatoes, sweet peas or edible flowers. The plants complete the cycle for us by making seeds to use for the next season.

There also is a thread of what I like to call my lazy gardener in this book. This kind of gardening doesn't have to be hard. In fact, if gardening feels like hard work, it no longer nurtures us and we have a tendency to shy away from it. Make the process fun and foster that feeling inside of you, then watch how it shows up in your garden.

Becoming an urban farmer only requires a shift in how we think. Rather than concentrating on a five-foot by ten-foot garden plot, step back and expand your vision to view the entire landscape as a palette for growing. Find all the nooks and crannies of your growing space and experiment to see what grows best in them.

Grow Wherever You Go is a compilation of my articles, research and personal experiences during the past 25 years. I begin with an exploration of the thinking process about how to create your own urban edibles, regardless of whether you live in an apartment or on acres of land. Then I delve into several inspirational stories of other people's successes, creative ideas and options for growing their own food. From the corporate executive growing fish on the balcony of his 6th floor condominium in Honolulu to an everyday couple that started their own urban farm on an original President Roosevelt's New Deal home site, everyone has something fascinating to share.

Urban Farm Possibilities

As farmlands become more scarce due to overuse and increased land development, the importance of growing food in our urban areas is increasing. Imagine developing gardens that become fully integrated, seamless parts of our society. Using urban spaces such as campuses, parks, road medians, housing developments, and of course our own front and back yards, to grow food — food grown by the community for consumption in the community.

What if we were to use these spaces and the resources that normally are used to care for non-edible plants and landscapes, to grow edibles such as fruit trees, herbs and vegetables? Ventures including urban farming and orcharding, community, roof-top and victory gardens, and backyard farming help us address our food-supply issues within urban areas and reestablish our essential connection to the source of our food. Given the significant environmental impact that public places have on the areas they occupy, and the vast resources they use and offer, it is crucial to consider how we can collaborate within urban communities in order to rethink food production.

Urban areas have long been used for agriculture in third world countries, with most urban farmers raising food out of necessity rather than desire. According to the United Nations, "about 800 million urban farmers provide about 15% of the world's food, and this proportion could be increased. Urban farmers in Hong Kong produce two-thirds of the poultry and almost half of the vegetables consumed by the city."

Urban farming models have been in existence for many thousands of years, but primarily have been practiced in third world countries. As first world countries come to a realization of the environmental impact of growing and shipping food, we will need to find alternative ways of raising food. Urban farming models can be a big part of the solution and we can start in our own back (and front) yards.

Shifting to Edibles

The notion of an edible landscape is actually quite simple. I like to say that if you are going to take the time and resources to nurture a plant you might as well make it edible. So that is what I have done — converted the flowerbeds and flowerpots of my home into a palatable mix of fresh fruit, vegetables, and herbs. Yes, it is THAT simple.

During the past 25 years, I have relentlessly explored urban sustainability and green living, which has repeatedly led me back to the garden and growing my own food. A few years ago my "garden" shifted in my mind to my "farm", which I have dubbed "The Urban Farm." Growing every imaginable vegetable, fruit and flower, has become a passion. My one-third-acre urban lot in a traditional neighborhood in the heart of Phoenix, Ariz. has become a community gathering place for urban dwellers who want to learn the process of transforming their everyday non-edible landscapes into ones that flourish with plenty of food.

When I arrived at the Urban Farm in 1989 there were plenty of non-food producing trees and lots of grass. I live on flood-irrigated property, which basically means that my yard is flooded 24 times per year with six inches of water. These water rights are left over from when my property used to be a commercial fruit orchard. In most cases, here in the Valley of the Sun, flood irrigated properties do a very good job of growing grass. I've returned this land to its roots by installing and expanding my flowerbeds, converting them to edibles, and replacing the non-edible trees with a nice variety of fruit and nut trees.

A visitor's perception of my urban farm shifts drastically in the first few moments of their visit. There are no long rows of corn and beans lining the front or back yard to greet them; quite the contrary

I have a nicely manicured yard, landscaped with fruits, vegetables and flowers.

I have enjoyed the added benefit of growing vegetables and herbs for my friend's restaurant. She is delighted to receive locally grown produce, which her patrons love, and I am more than happy with the exchange of her culinary magic that feeds me so well.

Another friend of mine regularly eats out of his yard. Every afternoon he wanders out in his front and back yards and hand selects a variety of flavors, brings them in, to slice, dice and puree them into exquisite food creations. One of his favorite salads starts with a generous amount of lettuce used as the base for lighter flavor. He then adds a healthy selection of produce such as kale, spinach, arugula, fennel, cabbage, radish, onions, kumquat, cilantro, and basil. He slices them into fine ribbons to make chewing easier, and tops off his culinary creation with edible Nasturtium flowers and an incredible dressing of olive oil, juiced orange, soy sauce and balsamic. It truly is an edible delight and he says growing it all himself is so fulfilling.

Once you jump in I think you will find unlimited opportunities to harvest fresh fruit, vegetables and herbs throughout the year. You also will be amazed at the variety of wonderful meals you can create with your newfound bounty.

Just Observe

Finding your garden is the first step. Start by standing back, taking a deep breath and observing. Writer, Bill Mollison calls it protracted observation — the process by which, over an extended period of time, we take in our surroundings and process what is there for us to see. The longer you look the more you can take in. Be creative.

Perhaps your garden is in your front or back yard, on a rooftop or balcony or even in just a few small pots on your windowsill. Observing takes time…take the time to envision your garden.

Here are some simple concepts to keep in mind as you observe:

- Observe your patterns. Where do you like to be in your garden? How do you interact with the space? Perhaps you can put the herb garden near the kitchen door where it is easily accessible. You don't want to put

your garden out back in a corner that you rarely visit, but rather in a place that keeps your attention.
- How many ways can you use something in your landscape? In other words, how many functions can each "something" serve? I recently built an outdoor kitchen, primarily to use the greywater that would normally go down the drain to water my landscape. Additionally, cooking outside is delightful, it is closer to the garden, the sink provides a place to rinse the vegetables, and cooking outside keeps the heat outside.
- External forces such as sun, light, wind, rain, and water play a significant role in the success of your garden. Carefully consider how they impact your garden and use that to your advantage. Can you redirect your rainwater and greywater to water your trees? Better yet, plant your trees near the rainwater runoff.

Observe where the afternoon sun is, how the water flows when it rains and in what direction the wind primarily blows.
- Watch for microclimates. A microclimate is a place in your garden that is inherently cooler or warmer than another. In Phoenix a warmer spot in my yard will allow me to grow tomatoes in the winter while a cooler place will not. How can you take advantage of the microclimates in your garden?
- Other things to observe include aesthetics, color, scale, diversity, balance, human scale, and whatever else strikes your fancy. Perhaps there is a particular beneficial bug that lives in your space, or your cucumbers grow in one spot but not another. Be creative, discover your space.

I have a good friend who I call Margaret the Condo Gardener. Her garden is quite the contrast from mine, but she will tell you that it is every bit as gratifying. Margaret lives on the second floor of a condominium complex in Phoenix and has no space to grow more than a pot full of herbs. Hungry for her own garden she visited the Urban Farm a few years ago, attended some of our classes and tours, and then volunteered to help plant and nurture the gardens at the Urban Farm in an effort to learn more. Margaret began dreaming about how she could create her own garden and started walking around her neighborhood to look for a suitable venue.

She made an interesting discovery...the alleys and streets in her neighborhood are lined with edible treasures such as figs, citrus, and other fruit. As a way to meet her neighbors, and possibly discover a garden plot for herself, she began asking permission to pick the fruit.

Then one day she stumbled across Meg's place — a backyard with a densely overgrown, five-foot by ten-foot garden plot. She had never met Meg and with some trepidation knocked on her door. Much to her delight, Margaret found a woman who was more than happy to share her garden space.

Meg even offered her gardening tools and tips on how to easily and inexpensively enrich the soil using steer manure, bone meal, and mulch. For Margaret, this was a dream come true. She finally had a place to reconnect with the earth and grow some heavenly greens, herbs and flowers that are more abundant than she could have imagined. And by sharing her leftover garden goodies she is carrying forward the tradition of sharing the surplus and inspiring others to do the same.

Whatever size your patch, pot, yard or farm, gardening provides a simple and satisfying way of renewing our connection with fresh food as well as creating a special sense of community. Recently, Margaret summed it all up when she said, "I am no longer a consumer and a bystander. I am a gardener!"

How creative can you get in finding and implementing your garden? From a small pot for herbs in the windowsill to converting the public flowerbeds (that are often left untended) in your apartment complex, be creative.

Who knows…maybe before long the old dog-run will be home to your new chicken coop.

Getting Started

When you begin the journey to discover your garden it is important to recognize what resources are available in your surroundings and how they fit into the different layers of your landscape. This requires some thought and planning but can be as simple as planting a tree, with a small shrub underneath and herbs under that. It is not just carving out a corner of your back yard to add a garden; it is observing the space to see what already exists that can help advance your garden. Is there a tree that provides afternoon shade, a roof that sheds excess rainwater, or a washing machine that spits out perfectly good greywater for you to water your landscape? Start to envision the different layers that you could incorporate.

For many years, I had this wonderful grapefruit tree in my backyard that shaded my back patio and outdoor kitchen. It was originally planted in the 1930's and thrived amazingly well, until its life came to an end in 2005. Unfortunately, I lost the sweet smell of the spring flowers, the pleasure of enjoying a fresh grapefruit for breakfast, not to mention the invaluable shade that the tree provided from the harsh Arizona afternoon sun. About the time that the tree began dying a grape vine started climbing up its trunk. Before long the grapes had taken over and recreated the shade that the tree had been providing. Now, instead of grapefruit I have a grape tree and harvest a very nice crop of grapes each year. Nature had provided the arbor - I stood back, observed and took the opportunity.

Building Healthy Soil

First and foremost, I would encourage you to make your garden organic. I have seen over and over again the impact of chemicals on an ecosystem. Essentially chemicals throw the ecosystem off balance. Then nature does her best to reestablish harmony, which often causes imbalances of its own. Work on creating a healthy environment and it will benefit both you and your plants in the long run. To that end the best thing that you can do is build healthy soil.

A significant piece of your landscape layers is the dirt under your feet. Once you have determined your preferred method of urban farming, building healthy soil is one of the most important factors necessary to grow a successful garden.

Healthy soil is a balanced mix of:
- dirt, which contains minerals from broken-down rock;
- organic material, like leaves, sticks, compost and mulch;
- living organisms like worms and microorganisms,
- air space, so your soil is not too compacted; and of course,
- water.

There are many ways to build healthy soil and creating compost is the key. If you have ever thought about the prospect of building a compost pile and been stopped before you even get started — don't despair. There are some easy alternatives to composting that I like to call non-composting, which include keeping chickens, worm composting, and sheet-mulching. These all require much less work or preparation for the same or better results, while providing you with plenty of great organic material for your soil.

My favorite way of non-composting is

to give the job to your chickens. I know — your first reaction is, "I can't keep chickens in my yard." Now I am not talking about roosters, just hens. They are very easy to keep, are effective at weeding and controlling bugs, eat your kitchen and yard scraps, provide lots of great compost material, and give you the added bonus of the occasional egg or two for your breakfast enjoyment.

Now if you aren't quite up for keeping hens, you might try worms, which are much more innocuous. They do their own kind of digging, provide their own kind of manure and do a really good job of munching on your kitchen scraps. They are as easy to keep as putting a bucket under your sink with some shredded newspapers and adding worms. Or, you can add an old bathtub in some corner of your yard and vermicompost away (the fancy word for worm composting).

Another favorite and fast way of adding oodles of organic matter to a garden is a process called sheet-mulching. This process is also the most cost effective way to create great soil in your garden. It takes a little work up front, but is well worth the effort. Sheet-mulching not only builds soil, but adds a thick layer of mulch to help retain water. If you are starting a garden from scratch, sheet-mulching gives you a jumpstart on your garden beds. Even if you've been gardening for years, this method boosts your bounty because you build your garden right on top of your existing soil. This process also appeals to the lazy-farmer in me because there is no need to dig.

Sheet-mulching is simple. Begin by selecting the area where you would like your garden and clear away any weeds or grass. Avoid putting a garden on Bermuda grass or other invasive weeds, as the weeds will reclaim the space very quickly. Next you will need to acquire potting soil, composted manure, and some kind of lightweight, dried organic material, such as leaves or hay. The hay and manure will be the bulk of the mulching material, while the potting soil permits you to plant seeds right away. Some choices for organic bulk material include leaves and alfalfa hay, which can be found by the bale at most feed stores. You also can keep an eye out for neighbors raking and bagging leaves.

Open the bales of hay or bags of leaves and fluff them in the area where you are putting your garden. You want to create a layer of organic material about six inches deep before adding a thin layer of manure. The manure will speed up the process of breaking down the hay and adds valuable nutrients to your garden. You can add layers to your heart's content, repeating the process, alternating organic material with manure, until you build sheet-mulched beds as thick as you desire. Natural processes will break down the layers to garden mulch over the next six months. The added bonus is that you can take your kitchen scraps and tuck them into this "layered" garden and let nature take over.

This process can be repeated on a yearly schedule until you are happy with the amount of soil you've gained. If you are using this process on a bed that has shrubs or trees, leave at least a six-inch gap between the mulch and the trunks of the plants.

Now comes the fun part...planting. Pick a place in your sheet-mulched garden, hollow out a bowl-sized area and fill it with some of your potting soil. You can plant your seeds directly into this soil bowl and they will flourish because this process provides water retention and breathing room for the roots. As the mulched area ages the plants will move down with the mulch and do just fine.

Non-composting is easy. It just takes a little effort to get it set up and working. At the Urban Farm compost happens with chickens, worms, sheet-mulching and composting. The fruits of my labor arrive in great-tasting food that I harvest almost every day of the year. Using one or all of these methods just about guarantees you a great crop. Remember though, composting takes time, as does raising a great garden. Be patient and compost away.

What's in a Seed?

Then there are the seeds. I once read a saying, "If one can live in their imagination then their life will be a dream come true." I've often wondered if that quote was inspired by a gardener. So many of us see a picture in our mind's eye of what we want to create as we plan our gardens. We pore over plant catalogs, gather treasured seeds from past harvests, and eagerly look forward to trying new seeds shared by our gardening friends. We contemplate the tiny white, black or brown ovals, spheres and dots and imagine how they will fulfill the promise of what they will become once planted in our gardens.

In an effort to clear up any seeds of confusion I will explain the three distinct "flavors" of seeds: heirlooms, hybrids and GMO's (genetically modified organisms). Heirloom seeds are left just as Mother Nature intended, while the hybrids and GMO's involve some level of human intervention.

Heirloom, or open-pollinated seeds as they are sometimes called, are seeds that have been passed from generation to generation and have stayed true to their ancestral roots by consistently producing the same offspring. This results in plants that genetically are hundreds or thousands of years old, each developing a resistance to the diseases and pests with which it evolved. When this type of seed is planted and allowed to grow and go to seed again, it will most always produce the same plant.

Seed banks serve a vital role in the preservation of the genetic diversity embodied in the heirloom species. Organizations such as The Southern Seed Legacy, Seed Savers International and Native Seed Search also have created methods to work with indigenous peoples to preserve such seeds. Of particular interest to me is the way Cornell University in Geneva, New York maintains an incredibly diverse collection of apple and grape plants, boasting over 2,500 apple cultivars and 1,300 grape cultivars.

Hybrid seeds have their own magic. I find that most people are familiar with the term hybrid, which is similar to the process that occurs in nature called natural selection. The process is simple: plant A cross-pollinates with plant B creating plant C. In essence this is how plants and animals slowly evolve. Here is where it gets interesting — about 150 years ago a gentleman named Gregor Mendel discovered that different pea plants (Pisum sativum) carried different traits and that by selectively breeding these plants he could bring out, or suppress, different traits. The value in this method is that the "positive" traits in a plant or animal can be brought out, while the "negative" traits can be suppressed.

So now on to real life…a farmer has a really sweet watermelon (A) but it has a lot of seeds, and a watermelon with a great shelf life (B.) By selectively breeding these two plants the farmer finds that the resulting watermelon magically doesn't have seeds, and he gets a sweet fruit with a long shelf life. The unfortunate part of this process is that hybridized plants either have no seeds or make seeds that are not viable for future generations. So saving seeds can be somewhat futile, and of course impossible with "seedless" watermelons.

I get a lot of questions from people who have concerns about GMO's. Currently these seeds are only available to commercial farmers and, as of this year, are *not* available at the nursery or in live plants that you can buy. For a great primer on this topic, see the book *Genetically Engineered Food: Changing the Nature of Nature*, by Martin Teitel & Kimberly Wilson.

Another term you may have seen applied to seeds is organic. Simply put, organic seeds are those that have been grown in a manner that is consistent with the U.S. Department of Agriculture's Organic Standards. There are organically grown heirloom and hybrid seeds. However, under the current organic guidelines you will not see organically grown GMO seeds because by definition they are excluded.

By carefully selecting and sowing your seeds your imagination's dream garden will become a reality. My strategy at the Urban Farm is to plant as many heirloom seeds as possible. That way when they go to seed nature carries the process forward. I usually spread the seeds directly and don't even bother collecting them for later as the seed knows when to sprout.

Urban Farming Models

There are many possible ways to experience your garden. Here are some examples of community growing models that have proven successful in some cities throughout the United States and are ripe for expansion in your own neck of the woods.

Victory Gardens

Victory gardens are a concept that was born during World War II to nurture home gardens and support the country's food supply. We were a country at war, suffering from commodity shortages that demanded a great deal of personal sacrifice. This simple concept drew our country together around a national crisis to create a grassroots sustainable system of farming — one that can be implemented in virtually everyone's yard. Even though this is an old concept it is regaining popularity in today's economic environment.

Community Gardens

Community gardens are public places where the community comes together and people can rent their own small garden plot. The garden, often run by a community organization or nonprofit, usually supplies tools, water, fertilizers, education and other resources while the gardener provides the labor and love. Community gardens represent a large part of city gardens and can represent a "return to a simpler life" by providing a place for the community to come together to work in harmony and learn.

Neighborhood Farms

This model is based on the concept of creating entire communities landscaped with food. Village Homes on 80 acres in Davis, CA, has been referred to as one of the world's best examples of sustainable development and has incorporated food throughout its entire development. Farming on this scale requires foresight and a huge commitment to sustainability and the community.

The Urban Farmer

Urban farmers make a concerted effort to grow and distribute food from their community garden, residential lot, or rooftop, typically growing specialty crops and staples for distribution in neighborhood restaurants and at local farmers markets. Their motivation usually stems from a desire to grow and share and not from a desire for riches. Urban farmers are a vital part in the urban farming model as they hold the passion for farming and tend to inspire and motivate others to grow their own food.

The abundance of fruit that one can grow never ceases to amaze me. In my yard alone, I grow a wide variety of herbs, sweet, navel and blood oranges, lemons, figs, peaches, and apricots as well as an abundance of root crops, squash and other vegetables.

Gleaning

Gleaning is the collection of unused or excess items, which can include fruits, vegetables, wood, and other items that would normally go to waste. For example, in central Phoenix, there are many areas that have stands of thousands of old citrus trees. Too often the fruit falls to the ground and rots. Gleaning addresses the collection and use of these resources by harvesting and distributing them for use elsewhere. In Phoenix, the West Side Food bank is one of the primary gleaners of excess citrus.

The U.S. Department of Agriculture has developed many gleaning programs outlined on their Web site, all of which are designed to collect leftover or unwanted food and distribute it to places of need.

Urban Orchards

As a culture we include trees and plants in our environment, from the medians in the streets, to parks, yards, office buildings and schools. The book *Growing Greener Cities: A Tree-Planting Handbook* states, "You may not realize it, but you are living in the midst of a forest. Every tree you see is linked to all the other trees and plants throughout the city. This delicate network is a living system that contributes to the well-being of our environment, cleansing and cooling the air, shading our streets, and beautifying the world we inhabit. We call this living, growing system 'the urban forest.' As we head into the twenty-first century, the role that trees play in our environment will become increasingly more important."

Nature lives all around us, making our task one of deciding how we can best utilize what nature has to offer. Implementing urban orchards addresses the replacement of these plantings with edible trees and shrubs, such as fruit and nut trees and berry bushes. The infrastructure already exists to manage these plants, as we already prune, water, and nurture non-fruiting species in our urban landscape. We simply need to make minor modifications in this structure to address food production and education. Often it's just a matter of informing the people involved as to the value of growing food crops in urban areas.

The Urban Farm Model

The Urban Farm Model incorporates many of the concepts described above. It combines a return to nature, education, community building and farming in the city. Model urban farms include: restaurants that use the produce grown on site, coffee/tea houses for socializing with friends, demonstration gardens, urban orchards, plant nurseries, seminars, education, seed collection and use, book and plant sales. Combining these concepts, the urban farm becomes a gathering place for the community.

Fairview Gardens in Golita, California is one such place. Over the past one hundred years the land around Fairview Gardens has developed into a heavily urbanized area characterized by dense row housing and urban concrete. The eleven acres that today comprise Fairview Gardens has been permanently preserved in an urban land trust. This urban farm helps enhance life in the community through education and food production as well as its international distinction as a model for urban farming. This model serves to bring communities together around community and food production like no other.

This Urban Farm Model takes each of these a step further and integrates the edible landscape model into the fabric of the place it occupies, both producing food and providing a forum for inspiring and educating visitors. Additionally, this model uses the processes of nature to most effectively take advantage of the climate and environment in which it lives. The urban farm also strives to seamlessly integrate food production into the landscape rather than keeping the expected 'farm/garden' separate. Through the integration of food production within the entire landscape, the utilization of onsite resources such as labor, creativity and teaching, plus the addition of the structure to manage the production of food, we are building a rich legacy that will support the local community.

Ready, Set…Grow

We have explored a process that takes you through discovering your own urban edibles whether you live in a condo or on a farm. It starts with being patient and observing what your surroundings have to offer, noticing where the sun, wind and rain impact your space and how you can best utilize them. Then we looked at how simple edible landscaping can be, from planting fruit trees to converting your flowerbeds to edibles and herbs.

My daily journey begins on any given spring morning — I am up at dawn, feeding the chickens, planting a garden bed with gladiolas, beans and squash, and harvesting fresh apricots, all before breakfast. This is my meditation before the day starts, my connection to Mother Earth, my interlude of fun before other responsibilities carve their way into my day. After 15 years of operating my own software company I decided to leave my work in technology and pursue my education, eager to turn my passion for urban farming in Phoenix, Ariz. into a living reality.

Phoenix is a city of approximately four million people. In the center of this urban sprawl, my house sits on a 1/3 acre lot. Nestled along my street are thirty houses, all built in the 1940's, all designed to resemble each other, yet over the decades all have taken on personalities of their own. On the paved street in front of my house, the neighborhood children play touch football and practice catch for their summer baseball league. Using my imagination, the noise from the nearby freeway sounds like the roll of the ocean along the California coast. In general, this is your stereotypical urban neighborhood.

However a few years ago, I decided to replace my entire landscape with edible plants. Perhaps you would call what I do here on the Urban Farm obsessive or even eccentric, I don't know. What I do know is that it has very deep roots in my life. A friend of mine believes that the earth breathed on me when I was a boy and left a passion that seeps through my veins. Maybe that is true.

I have always known that there is something inherently wrong with the way that we choose to live on the planet, using and abusing the resources that reside here as though there is no tomorrow. From a very early age I sensed a nudging in my heart that convinced me that something should be done to raise our consciousness. So, over the years I have explored many ways of lightening our footsteps on the planet. Creating opportunities to raise this awareness became and remains my mission. As you can tell I am quite the storyteller and throughout my books I have inserted tales of garden successes and failures. So, when it came time to ponder what stories I would tell you next I envisioned digging deeper into my history to share some simple things you could do to create your own urban farm.

However, as I did this and chatted with others, I discovered that there are many people working toward urban food production. So, I reached out to my community and asked them to share their inspirational stories of garden bliss. I am sure that you will find them as inspiring as I did. Additionally, you can enjoy the online resources that accompany many of the stories — pictures, additional content and videos for your growing pleasure. Visit UrbanFarmPress.com to see these stories come alive.

Grow Wherever You Go!

I Am an Urban Farmer
By Carol Bennett
Tempe, AZ

I used to be an "urban gardener," having a small garden everywhere I've lived from New Jersey to Minnesota, and now Arizona.

I now consider myself an "Urban Farmer". The difference? Today I view my entire 1/3 acre urban yard as potential space for raising food. I have planted three apple trees, and have plans for figs and peaches. My front flowerbed that used to have petunias now contains an artichoke for food and marigolds for three reasons: color, to bring in pollinators, and to act as a pest repellent. Learning about the Urban Farm was the turning point for me, combined with all the scares about fresh produce during the past two years. I am determined to grow as much of my own food as I can.

My Fire Escape Garden
Mike Lieberman
New York City

My garden started in the spring of 2009 out of a deep desire to reconnect with my food supply. It seems like we just think of produce as "growing" in the grocery store, and lost perspective on how our food really grows. I was reading a book on eating locally and was amazed to learn that, on average, food travels up to 2,000 miles from the farm to our tables. Since I eat a lot of fresh vegetables and fruits I wanted to cut down on my food budget and get better connected with my food.

I joined my local CSA (Community Supported Agriculture) and started going to farmer's markets, but even that food is grown far away or treated with pesticides. So I started reading more and asking for information from the growers at the farmer's markets. You might think this is crazy, considering I live in an apartment in New York City, but it all came together when I discovered self-watering containers that I could make to fit in a space as small as my fire escape landing.

I made modified versions of what I saw online and was able to make them out of mostly recycled materials in 20 to 30 minutes for under $5. Plus I make planters out of coffee cans, gallon jugs and two liter soda bottles. I cut off the bottom part of the soda bottles, reinforce them with duct tape and hang them on the fire escape railing. All of this has been done within fire code and apartment regulations. Now I enjoy kale, Swiss chard, lettuce, sweet peppers, chili peppers, cherry tomatoes, basil, apple mint, Greek oregano and parsley.

When you really think about it, food is essential to our lives and I want fresh, real food, not the great science experiment that we call processed or GMO'd food. I was told that food has changed more in the last 50 years than it did in the 1,000 years prior. I didn't go to school or get a fancy certificate, and I'm not preachy, but I like to show people how easy and really delicious it is to grow some of their own fresh, pesticide free food…even on a fire escape!

****

1933 New Deal
By Robert Ray
Phoenix, AZ

My wife Bea and I have lived in the Phoenix Homesteads Neighborhood on a quarter acre lot for 16 years. We have never been sure what to do with our yard. It has gone through many transformations and has never been finished.

In the midst of our country's financial crisis my wife and I, like a lot of people, were wondering how we could survive in a depressed economy. It occurred to us that the Phoenix Homesteads community in which we live was the product of the depression era New Deal — small homes built on larger lots to facilitate people supplementing their income by growing some of their own food.

We jumped right in and dug a 10' x 20' garden on the South side of our patio and had it planted by October 15th. Our winter garden did fabulously well with all kinds of lettuce, spinach, kale, mustard greens, turnips, beets, carrots, peas, garlic, celery, and various herbs (we supplied everyone we knew with cilantro for their salsa.) For some reason we didn't have any onions even though we planted plenty. We needed to learn more. We have taken gardening and green living classes offered around town. With the knowledge we have gained we are now composting as well as harvesting rainwater, and recently we've acquired a culvert that we will convert into a rain storage cistern.

Our spring garden (a 16' x 16' plot in the middle of our back yard) did really well with the zucchini, watermelon, cantaloupe, and tomatoes doing extraordinarily well. We have just finished planting our gardens for the winter — the 10' x 20' to the south, the 16' x 16' in the middle of the back yard, and the tomatoes along a South facing wall on the North side of the yard, plus a brand new 10' x 10' plot in the front yard full of salad ingredients.

I am currently enrolled in a Permaculture Design Course and every day I have a better idea of what to do with our yard. I am very excited about espaliering four fig trees along our back fence, all of which were grown from cuttings. Next year I'm going to start a Belgian Fence of apple trees to shade our tomatoes.

Returning Home
By Jennifer Olsen
Raytown, MO

I started down the urban farming road because I was touched, inspired, and motivated by the growing movement, and it was not new for me. I grew up with mud squishing through my toes and my mama canning her own veggies, but got away from it for a while. Then one day I happened upon a copy of Mother Earth News in the lobby of the local community center. I LOVED it and once again felt at home.

Urban farming made sense to me as a way to be in touch with where my food comes from, but more importantly it speaks to my need of staying near a city. Why wait until I buy a rural property to take a stab at becoming more self-sufficient? I loved the idea of having the best of both worlds and using what you have in a non-traditional way.

I took a class on building rain barrels. I toured other urban farms and gardens for designs, hints, and relationships. This led to adventures in worm composting (can't believe I converted this squeamish, girlie girl to a worm handler) and other joys of growing my own. Even though I had my own space I joined the local community garden because of the free rototiller, community interaction, and other perks. I sought out a local program to become a master gardener, subscribed to a couple of homesteading blogs, and, oh yeah, purchased a property that is my dream with a HUGE yard of almost half an acre. The property already had three persimmons, one apple, and a mature black walnut tree. Additionally, I have added a dwarf lemon tree, a blueberry, and a raspberry bush.

The neighborhood had unused resources appropriate to forage, including crabapples and other fruit that was disregarded and rotting on the ground. I was well on my way. I immediately put in as many raised beds as I could from salvaged materials. I went for the organic-style garden and all heirloom varieties. It just felt so natural letting the plants go to seed so I could save them for the following year. I joined Seed Savers Exchange. I dried. I froze. I canned. The harvest was good. I am amazed at how little apple butter comes from a huge amount of apples (even though it was extraordinarily tasty). I even made dilled green bean pickles from our green beans. Each experience was one of learning.

Not all of it went well. I tried making my own sauerkraut from my cabbage, but it was so disgusting that I was afraid to even try it. And then there was the mulch that I bought that was infested with termites!! Yikes!

It is funny how everything is always in a state of "in progress." The chicken coop hasn't come into fruition, a new roof was more important. No dairy goats yet either.

And my fantasies for composting toilets will just have to be that for now. My desire for alternative/renewable energy has come down to one small purchase a month. First it was stoves, lanterns, etc. in case the power went out. Then I progressed to a crank radio/lantern, a solar lamp, a solar IPOD/cell phone charger, solar rechargeable batteries, solar fan, and more. I figure if I keep 'unplugging' away at it, eventually it will add up to a lower electric bill.

Just today, I turned an entire bushel of apples into my first batch of cider. In the past, I brewed mead and dandelion wine, but cider is a whole new adventure. And that is just what I like — a new adventure, something new to learn, a richer understanding of life, the earth and my place on it.

My neighbors view me as a bit of an oddity. The fact that I also like to mosaic anything that doesn't move probably doesn't help. They are mostly older and think it is funny that a single mother does these things. They traipse over and peer at my little operation and we discuss what I consider are the dying arts. Not a one of them can believe I don't use any chemicals, regular fertilizers or pesticides (I offered to let them sniff my fish emulsion, but no one would.) I try hard not to let them know what has come from dumpster diving as I live in a really nice neighborhood. I do take them fresh baked bread as often as I can to keep them on my good side, hoping they remember the bread if I mess up my compost and stink them out. And on the day that I bring home a goat — I'll take over two loaves and some homemade jam to boot. We'll see...

Asbury Community Refugee Garden
By Kelli M. Donley
Phoenix, AZ

While attending a socially conscious church, I listened as stewardship committee members bemoaned unfunded dreams of solar panels, grey water projects, and eliminating the acre of Bermuda grass surrounding the church. While I didn't have the funding to turn Asbury United Methodist Church – built in the early 1900s – into a green building, I did have an idea for that grass.

What if we turned the church lawn into a community garden that could reach out to local refugee families living in the neighborhood? Our church is regional – most of the congregants live far away and drive into the city to attend Sunday services. One of our biggest concerns is our lack of connection with the immediate neighborhood.

To determine if the congregation was

interested in reaching out, we started with an "adopt a tree" campaign, selling citrus trees for a small orchard. In no time I'd sold far more than the initial goal of 25 trees. The congregation was certainly behind the idea of a community garden. The next step was how to find interested farmers?

Professionally, I work with a nonprofit that helps newly arrived refugee families develop social and educational skills in their new hometown. I contacted some of my colleagues and within a few weeks, we had more than a dozen countries represented at our tree-planting day. Congregants with children running between their legs speaking in a cacophony of languages, planted trees and noted with tears in their eyes that such diversity (and obvious hunger) lived within eyesight of the church.

Within a few weeks, after an incredible burst of support from my friends and family, I distributed more than 500 seed packets to eight refugee families. With more than half an acre available for their use and divided among the participants, we relied on donated tools and the church's grandfathered water rights to make this grassy lawn into a secure food source. We "dug in" both physically and metaphorically.

The project is now in its second planting season, and while I'd love to say it has been entirely smooth sailing, we've had some considerable hurdles. Refugees are financially unstable and statistically prone to moving frequently. This leaves garden plots planted and abandoned. The importance of heirloom seed, organic gardening, and supporting local community projects are lost when they are in survival mode. So, for many of our farmers, going to the grocery store makes more sense.

Another challenge we've encountered includes a lack of planning on my part. Those 500 seeds packets were a wonderful gift, but were not the most appropriate way of determining what we'd grow. Instead, we'll use the Arizona planting calendar for the next round and ensure we are selecting items that grow well with irrigation.

Truly the biggest challenge that we've met with this project is the invasive weed—Bermuda grass. I'm entirely convinced the devil in the Garden of Eden wasn't a snake; it was a tall, lengthy branch of mischievous Bermuda grass that wrapped itself around all it could.

We were trying to keep the garden organic, but the truth is, to make this land viable for gardening, we need to kill the grass. Solarization hasn't worked because the irrigation still comes in and it destroys the plastic. So, we've decided to do one round of weed killer before we plant next time. The county extension office has assured me this is not the type that will remain in the earth for seven years. We are crossing our fingers that we can get rid of this horrible weed and replace it with something much more fruitful.

The end result of our first growing season was more than 100 pounds of okra, planted by a Burundian family that moved. Making lemonade out of okra isn't easy, but after consulting the gardening guru Google, I learned pickled okra can be quite tasty; 16 quarts later, we aren't having a bake sale at church. We're selling okra to fund a new season of seeds.

So, with those 24 citrus trees growing each day (one died), we are pushing forward with a new plan. We've divided the land between two families who are being selected through an interview process. They must make their commitment known. We will then focus our efforts on these two families, the crops they plant and their social needs for 6 months. After their first growing season, we'll reevaluate and they may very well keep the land for another season. We've also secured an agreement with a local Farmer's Market to sell additional produce, providing further financial support to refugee participants.

We hope this new formula will be more appropriate to see the Asbury Community Garden blossom. We've got plans to plant for many more fruit trees this spring. Bringing together the church and community to improve food security for hungry families makes great sense to me.

****

My Instant Garden
By Parri Willie
Phoenix, AZ

When I was a little girl we lived in New Jersey, and my mom always had a garden — growing green beans and tomatoes among other things. I can remember going out in the summer months and picking the beans and eating them right where I picked them. When I was 25 I moved to Phoenix. Living in the "desert" I didn't think it was possible to recreate that garden. And then, 2 years ago, after a tour of the Urban Farm I realized it is VERY possible.

My home is a typical Phoenix tract home in a development where every house has colored rock for a yard. To remove the rock and dig up the ground underneath seemed like a huge undertaking and then I could only hope that the dirt there would sustain a garden. It would be much more practical and successful, I thought, to build a raised garden and fill it with proper soil and compost.

Planning to build a raised-bed garden that was 5 feet wide by 10 feet long and 12 inches deep, I enlisted the help of a friend and we purchased three nice quality pieces of pine, 10 feet long by 2 inches wide 12 inches tall and enough brackets and screws to hold all the sides together. We cut one of the boards in half for the 5 foot ends of the garden and then connected the four sides together securely with the brackets. After raking away much of the rock from our selected area, we set this outer "shell" of our garden down, made sure it was level and then filled it with a mixture of organic soil and compost. After planting my chosen vegetables, I wrapped a wall of chicken wire around the outside of the garden to protect my veggies from our little rabbit visitors. This garden project was fairly easy, cost under $100, and took less than a day to put together.

This past summer I successfully grew tomatoes, zucchini, strawberries and green beans, and, yes, I picked the beans and ate them right there in the yard. Some sections of the garden didn't grow as well as others so I spent time fertilizing and moving the soil around a bit before getting the fall garden planted. I expect to harvest red and yellow onions, broccoli, sweet peas, eggplant, tomatoes, 2 kinds of lettuce, spinach and carrots as my winter crop.

Part of the thrill of having my garden is the sense of accomplishment in seeing the plants grow and produce food, but a bigger part is knowing that I am feeding my family healthy, organic food that is full of nutrients and free of pesticides and chemicals. I can definitely see adding another garden box at a later date and doubling my harvest!

****

Pool Side Fish Farmer
By Robert Gilsdorf
Phoenix, AZ

When the last of my five kids entered high school I found that no one was using the swimming pool in the back of our one-acre yard in the old Arcadia orchard area of Phoenix. I had two gardens that were doing well with the compost from the yard and since the kids did not keep up the pool maintenance, I decided to raise fish in it. I could use the backwash system for irrigation and fertilization of the gardens and also grow surface plants for additional composting material. I purchased fingerling catfish from a fish farmer in Verde Valley and tilapia fingerlings from a mail-order farm in Arkansas. Every fall I would order about 1000 fingerlings, after harvesting the previous year's crop of about 100 pounds of catfish and tilapia fillets.

The transformation process was simple — I cut a trench across the pool deck from the Jacuzzi to the pool and circulated the water from the bottom of the pool to the Jacuzzi, which acted as a settling tank for the fertile muck that accumulated. Then once a month I backwashed it from the Jacuzzi into the gardens.

I had some difficulty catching the fish and eventually found I had to drain the pool and net out the large ones. My costs were small: the fish fingerlings and the feed. I calculated that I raised fish fillets for about 74 cents a pound. However, there was that little additional cost of beer and cigars for the guys and girls who came over to clean the fish the night before the annual neighborhood "Bayou Bob's Fish Harvest Party". My bonus consisted of great community, wonderful gardens, and enough fish for an "all-you-could-eat" fish fry.

I retired and sold the house to my daughter and her seven kids who needed a pool for their summers in Phoenix. So, the pool was returned to its original crystal clear blue state. I recently built a small addition to the house, so my wife and I can visit for six months of the winter. This spring I'll be putting in a large garden where I plan to put in grapes for wine!

Balcony Fish Farming
By Matt Johnson
Kakaako, HI

When I moved into my condo three years ago in Kakaako, Hawaii, everything was great. I had easy access to a pool, hot tub, gym, mini-marts, bars, and the beach. Who could ask for anything more? Well, I decided that these modern conveniences were not enough and, in fact, I did need more. More green, more life, more non-concrete creations. A fortunate part of my living situation is that my condominium has a 400-square-foot patio. I decided to use this space to try my hand at urban farming with the goal of growing an entire meal just 20 feet from my kitchen. I am happily a carnivore, so I knew that in order to make a meal that I would truly enjoy I would need to have some type of meat. Chicken, beef, pork, and goat were out the question, even though I did think about it. However, there was no way to get around the condo by-laws that stated "no farm animals". I decided fish was my only option. I also wanted greens to make a salad. So, with my end goal of a dinner of fish and salad in mind, I decided aquaponics was exactly what I needed.

As defined by Wikipedia, aquaponics is "the symbiotic cultivation of plants and aquatic animals in a recirculating environment." Basically, it's combining hydroponics with aquaculture in a closed-loop system that uses the fish-fertilized water to fertilize the plants. The plants then filter the water, which is deposited back into the fish tank.

Fortunately, my business allows me to work with all different types of farmers on Oahu; luckily one of them is an aquaculture expert and another grows hydroponic lettuce. Both were willing to help me along the way. I found someone who was going out of business and was able to pick up a couple of 60-gallon fish tanks for

$50 each. Granted, you could use something as simple as a five-gallon bucket, but I wanted something bigger. Next, I took hydroponic growing tubes and put them above the fish tanks, pointing down so that water flowing through the tubes would pass over the roots and fall in to the tanks at the end. The third part of the system is the sump tank, located underneath the fish tanks. As water enters the fish tank from the hydroponic growing tubes above, it causes the water to overflow into a three-foot-long pipe located at the middle of the tank. The pipe gravity feeds the water to a sump tank located underneath the fish tanks. In the sump tank there is a 1.5 HP (Hayward Pump) water fountain pump that shoots the water up through a hose four feet where it connects to one half-inch PVC pipe. The pipe distributes water to each of the hydroponic tubes through skinny straws. This completes the closed loop system.

After I finished building the tank

stands out of 4 x 4's and plywood (total cost of $50), it was time to find some fish.

Tilapia is the most commonly used fish due to its ease of raising. I started with six, per tank, that I harvested from a friend's pond in Hawaii Kai, 20 minutes from downtown Honolulu. When putting fish into your tanks you need to make sure you have enough fish to create enough nutrients, but also not so many that the water becomes toxic to the fish. A rule of thumb to try and follow is two pounds of fish per cubic foot of water.

Another factor to consider is aeration, which helps the fish with breathing since they are enclosed in a relatively small area. I use an air pump that allows me to attach two hoses, one for each tank. I attached an air-stone to each hose and then dropped it into each tank. To propagate the seeds, I use a sponge like medium, insert seeds into the growing medium, add water and in a few days, I have baby Swiss chard.

To date, I have successfully grown

manoa lettuce, mesculin, Swiss chard, kale, parsley, and arugula. Within sixty days, most of the different types of lettuce are ready to harvest. Depending on the amount of feed given to the tilapia, the fish can be ready to harvest in 3-6 months.

After about three months of trial and error — lettuce dying because of not enough water and a few tilapia dying because they jumped out of the tank — my dream of eating an entire meal that had been grown on my balcony came to fruition. I harvested two heads of butter lettuce, some Swiss chard, and caught two tilapia. Before cooking the fish, they spent a few hours in clean water to help rinse them out before cleaning. I rolled the fillets in flour and threw them in a hot pan with butter. The lettuce was rinsed and I added yellow-pear tomatoes that I harvested from a recycled bath tub that I use to grow various produce. My girlfriend brought over some wine and we had an enjoyable dinner for two.

It is My Little Garden of Eden
By Beverly Fizzell
Phoenix Arizona

When I moved to the foothills on the north side of South Mountain, I left behind a great garden in the farmland of Chandler, not knowing what a challenge the sand and rocks would be at the new place. We have a half-acre on a slope and there is no organic matter in the soil. After longing to get my hand in rich black soil again, we built a nine-foot by fourteen foot attached greenhouse on the southwest side of our house. It is right off the kitchen and my computer desk looks out into it. I admire my garden while I work.

I make great soil for the raised bed by composting 50% goat manure and 50% sawdust, which is available in abundance respectively from a small goat dairy and my husbands' workshop. Other composting starts in the kitchen where every single degradable food item goes into a container in the sink. I have a large plastic worm bin in the greenhouse where those scraps go and the bin is loaded with great healthy worms and topped with shredded recycled paper.

I feed worms, sow bugs, crickets, and other insects from the beds, to a large Cichlid fish in a 100-gallon stock tank that lives in the greenhouse. Occasionally I dump nutritious water from the tank on the raised bed. I use tree frogs and turtles for insect control and don't ever use pesticides, although I am tempted when there are white flies ruining my plants. A yellow card, coated with salad oil, traps them then magically ants come along and take the white flies off of the card. I believe ants are only pests when they are in the kitchen; otherwise they turn and aerate the soil. An old-time-gardener friend says, "Soil is soil unless it is on the floor and only then it is dirt. When you sweep it outside, it is then soil again."

A laundry sink drains into a flowerbed

outside. There is a small heater for the winter and an evaporative cooler in the summer. The water system is on a timer and drips from the ceiling like rain, much easier to take care of than watering lines lying on top of the beds. I can even go away for a few days and leave it. Water from the cooler bleeds off and drains into a basin from which coyotes, javelina, rabbits, squirrels, birds and bees drink. The overflow continues on out to a large (well watered I might add) eucalyptus tree. I have yet to try fruit trees outside, but would love to have citrus and peaches. It is much dryer and windier here than in town and plants outside suffer. The wildlife eats every single thing I plant outside, except lantana. The only safe place for plants is in the greenhouse.

I am growing bell peppers, tomatoes, eggplant, basil, beets, Swiss chard, bok choy, strawberries in hanging baskets and lots of flowers, including water lilies in the bowl of the fountain. There are numerous pots on the windowsills and shelves with flowers and other plants. Shelves are the wire ones from the hardware store and are suspended on chains from the ceiling. In the summer I cover the roof with a shade screen and it is ordinarily less than 90 degrees F in the greenhouse. Tomatoes can grow really tall, especially with the inadequate light, and can be trained to climb up a string that is attached to the ceiling and then tied across the rafters. I try to not plant too much of any one thing. Once I had three bell pepper plants that grew to the ceiling and I had to take off a screen and climb in the window to get the peppers.

There is something to eat from my greenhouse every single day of the year, even if it is just a handful of basil!

Ready, Fire, Aim
By Fern Richardson
Cypress, CA

For the longest time I didn't garden at all. Not because I didn't want to, or because I didn't know how, but because I kept on putting it off. I wanted to wait until I could have my dream garden surrounding my dream house. I kept telling myself that when I graduated from law school... when I passed the bar... when I got a job... After all those things happened, I would be able to buy a house with a yard.

When my plans didn't materialize I realized how silly it was to put off doing something until I could do it perfectly. I was missing out on all the satisfaction I could be having by tending a container garden on my apartment patio solely because it wasn't the type of garden I daydreamed about. I think a lot of things are like that. We never get around to accomplishing our goals — like living "green" or growing our own food — because it seems overwhelming or impossible. But by limiting ourselves to only doing something 100%, we miss out on all the benefits we'd get by doing the best we can and doing things slowly.

As soon as I had that epiphany, I never looked back. I bought some pots, flowers, and a peach tree and set to work filling my patio with plants. I've always mixed ornamental plants with edible plants because I wanted my garden to be beautiful and useful. It has worked out really well because the flowering plants attract lots of beneficial insects that help pollinate my edible plants, and keep pests under control. I now grow several different types of peppers, tomatoes, strawberries, peaches, apples, and tons of herbs. All in pots, located right outside my front door.

I'm all in favor of a "ready, fire, aim" approach to gardening. I've always loved plants, but I've never taken a class, and I certainly don't have a horticulture degree. I learned by reading magazines, books, websites, and asking for help from seasoned gardeners. There are great online gardening communities that I turn to for information and help. And of course, I learned a lot through trial and error!

Growing things that I can eat is incredibly rewarding, not to mention a lot of fun! Many fruits and vegetables taste better when they're home grown. Tomatoes taste a million times better when you're eating a fresh, off-the-vine variety that was developed for its good taste and not its ability to last a long time in a supermarket display. There also are a lot of things that are easy to grow in a pot that you just can't find at the supermarket. I grew lemon, lime, cinnamon, and purple varieties of basil this past season. A supermarket would never carry those.

When you actually start growing your own food, you're forced to confront what you think about chemical pesticides pretty early on. Growing fruits and vegetables is a guaranteed way to attract all sorts of insects. It's very frustrating to see a caterpillar eat an entire lettuce seedling in an afternoon, and the nearly instinctual reaction is to spray something on that sucker to kill it eight times over. But when you look at the ingredients in pesticide, they just scream "carcinogen." And if you buy the chemical pesticide anyway, the smell of the spray usually produces instant buyer's remorse. You just know something that smells like *that* isn't something you'd want to eat.

I tried using chemical pesticides when I first started my container garden, but I quickly decided that I'd rather have less than perfect fruits, vegetables, and herbs than ingest any of those chemicals, or accidentally get them on my skin when applying the spray. I try to practice good gardening techniques — like companion planting, attracting and supporting beneficial insects, and watering and fertilizing properly — that keep pests under control. I've also learned a lot about organic and natural ways to treat pest infestations, such as using Bt *(Bacillus thuringiensis - pesticide)* and insecticidal soaps. I'm not judgmental about other people's choices, but I know that for me, controlling pests organically was the right decision and an easy one to make.

In the years ahead, I look forward to learning more about growing my own food, organic fertilizers and pest control, and trying new things, like canning and preserving some of my harvest. I've also been investigating community gardens. They seem like a great way to expand my gardening space and meet fellow gardeners while I'm waiting on that dream house with a yard to materialize.

Grow Wherever You Go!

My Urban Year-Round Herb Garden
Karen Looney
Kansas City, MO

I am a pretty good cook and experimenting with new recipes in the kitchen is one of my favorite past times. I love using fresh herbs, but was frustrated with the lack of selection, their freshness, and of course the outrageous cost. This inspired me to take matters into my own hands.

I have lived in my home almost 10 years and have gardens planted around most of the foundation. This creates a challenge for growing edibles though because my house was built in 1929 and there is a real threat of DTD and lead paint in the soil, which is not "good eats" as Alton Brown says. So, how would I grow things to eat with the limited amount of property I had left, especially since most of it was either in front yard, viewable to the street, or tackled in the back by "Tulip," my 60-pound pit bull?

The answer...a portable herb garden in pots and a little strip by the driveway. In a space that tapers from five feet at the widest, down to two feet at the small end, with a length of ten feet, I put in more than 40 different plants. I wanted to experiment with different types of the same herbs, so I planted them in groups and doubled them up in pots. I created a variety of levels and looks to make the garden visually interesting. Because the garden was compact it was a cinch to keep weeded and cared for. Any time I created a dish, I just walked out to pick the herbs to finish it. The best thing about the garden though was how much that pretty little space cheered me up every time I came home.

Here in Kansas City, we get all four seasons in equal measure, so leaving tender plants outside means you have to keep buying new ones each year. In the fall, I pruned back the entire garden by a full one-third to get the plants ready to harden off and move inside for the winter. I dried the cuttings, made oodles of pesto, and put up six different kinds of herb vinegars for myself and as gifts for the holidays. With a couple of tables and two florescent grow lights in the basement, I can winter most types of herbs. I have rosemary that is spending its fourth year inside for the winter. The plants cheer up a pretty drab basement and I can still use the herbs to cook with all year long!

****

Eating Wild
By Greg Peterson
Phoenix, AZ

Edible landscaping can extend way beyond your yard and into the surrounding community and wild areas. Explore the public and wild spaces and see what you find. Recently I traveled to a friend's house north of Tucson. She lives on 20 acres and has spent the last three decades nurturing back to nature. Her works are works of passion, ones to restore the desert to its pristine self. Work done over decades repairing the damage of men and cattle. Mostly what she does is sculpture the land so that the water goes into the soil rather than run off. Rainwater harvesting is what it is called and it involves storing rainwater in the soil, preserving the much-needed moisture for the roots of parched desert plants and creating a dense thicket of desert forest.

I had come to Barb's for her annual Saguaro fruit harvest and generally to be away from my life — the constant going, never slowing down. Mostly my days consist of getting up by five am and working on my Urban Farm, eating breakfast, running off to write, to work for seven hours then home to finish incomplete projects at the farm.

This work schedule comes out of my deep commitment to change the way humans interact with nature. Daniel Quinn speaks about the best way to change the world -- not by putting programs in place with rules for people to follow -- but to change the way people think. My goal each day is to change people's minds about how we relate and interact with nature.

What I sometimes forget is that I too am able to have my mind changed, even when I am not looking. When I arrived, Barbara took me to visit a Palo Verde tree that was full of edible seeds. It seemed as though I was at the beginning of a ride that would change my mind about desert edibles forever. Up to that point my concept of desert edibles was confined to the prickly pear jam my mom used to make when I was a kid.

Before long I was eating the hulled seeds of Palo Verde, a pea shaped morsel the size of an edamame soy bean and about the same consistency. We then picked mesquite seed pods which, when boiled, turned into a thick syrup similar to maple but when milled became a wonderful, aromatic, gluten-free flour.

And the topper was our little excursion out in the early morning hours with 18-foot poles with wire hoops on the end in hand. We were off to harvest saguaro fruit, a tasty bright red fruit that lives at the top of the saguaro, some so tall that they even dwarfed our 18-foot pole.

Two tricks I learned about harvesting saguaro fruit: first, use the pole, which takes a lot of practice, to lasso the fruit and pop it away from the cactus bud; second, have someone ready, 18 feet below the fruit, to catch it. The fruits themselves are two to four inches long, torpedo shaped and pale green with a red hue to them.

It seems as though my mind has been changed. Now, I sit here in anticipation of the next trip to Barbs and the new discoveries that I will make eating her yard.